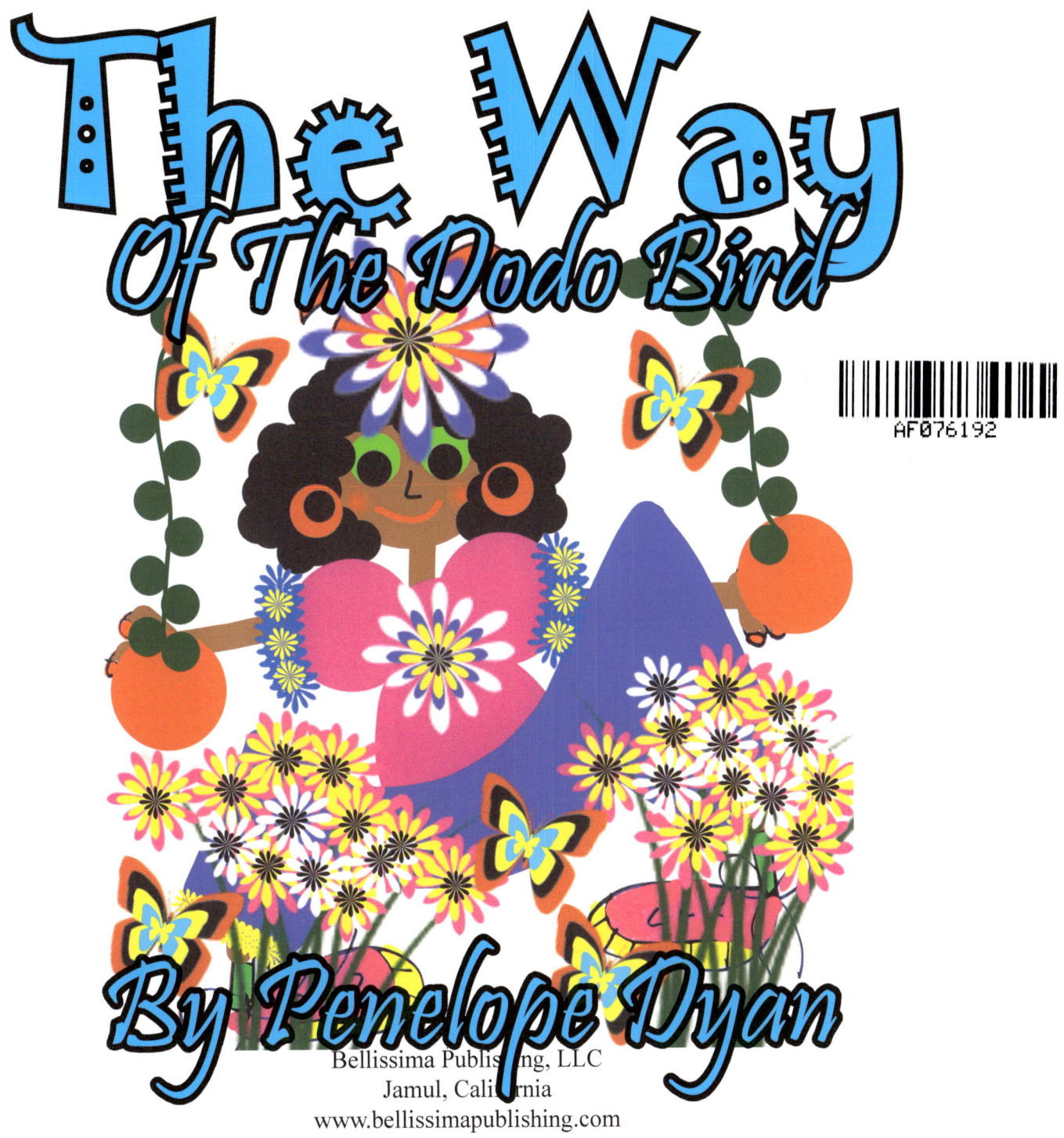

The Way Of The Dodo Bird

By Penelope Dyan

Bellissima Publishing, LLC
Jamul, California
www.bellissimapublishing.com

Copyright © 2021 by Penny D. Weigand

All rights reserved. No part of this book may be
reproduced or transmitted in any form or by any means,
electronic or mechanical, including photocopying,
recording, or by any other means, or by any information or
storage retrieval system, without permission from the publisher.

ISBN 978-1-61477-547-8
First Edition

"Having dominion over the creatures
of the world, means that
we need to take care of the creatures of the world"

PENELOPE DYAN

Introduction

Research tells us extinctions have been a natural part of our world's evolution Shockingly, it is estimated that more than 99% of the four billion species evolved on Earth are extinct. And (most importantly) it is also estimated that at least nine hundred went extinct in the just last five hundred years. And this is why we absolutely need to ask ourselves how we can protect this planet, because protecting this planet means we are also protecting ourselves. And if we don't act to protect this planet, we could also become extinct, just like the dodo bird! See: https://ourworldindata.org/extinctions

Think about this as you have fun practicing your reading skills and building your reading word vocabulary using this fun, 'learn to read' book, written and illustrated by award winning author, attorney and former teacher, Penelope Dyan, that is filled with word recognition, word repetition and rhyme, all included to help make learning fun!

And when you are all finished traveling through the pages of this book, you can go to Bellissimavideo's YouTube channel and you can watch the free, fun music video that goes with this book for even more learning fun!

Stop all of the madness!
Because if we don't do THAT . . .
haven't you heard?
We could (quite simply)
simply ALL go the way
of the extinct dodo BIRD!
You see, it is exactly as my mother said,
when she tucked me oh so tightly
(last night)
into my nice warm bed . . . . She said,
"We need to protect
ALL of the creatures of this world,
before we ALL go extinct
like the dodo BIRD!"

The elephant agreed
with my dear, sweet mother;
AND she said what my mother told me
was one hundred percent
absolutely TRUE!
AND since the elephant
never, never, EVER lies,
I would (quite simply) simply
listen to . . . AND believe the elephant
if I just happened to be YOU!
After all, she has known
for oh so very, very VERY long
that the woolly mammoth
HAS (quite simply)
simply been long, long, long GONE!

The oh so tall giraffe told me
that (with this) he absolutely
AND one hundred percent
(quite simply)
simply really, truly did AGREE!
AND so did the monkey
that sits oh so high, high, HIGH up
in the old, old OLD apple tree!

The smiling cow told me that she
absolutely AND one hundred percent
really, truly did (quite simply)
simply AGREE!
AND so did the sheep!
And . . . just in case you haven't heard,
someone ELSE who told me
that they ALSO agreed
with my mother
was their very, very, VERY best friend,
the happily, happily, happily,
oh so happily, chirping bird!

The prancing horse told me
that he (quite simply) simply
AND absolutely
one hundred percent
with my mother
really, truly did agree!
AND so did the hippopotamus,
and the busily buzzing bumble bee!

AND my father
agreed with all of the rest;
because it was, and is, and happens
to BE very, very, VERY clear
that he (quite simply}
simply knows my mother
always, always, ALWAYS knows
exactly what is BEST!

The mermaid,
and ALL of the fish in the sea,
told me that with mother
they also (quite simply)
simply and absolutely,
AND one hundred percent,
really, truly did AGREE!

And my very, very, VERY best friend
told me that she also
(with my mother)
really truly did AGREE . . .
right along with
the elephant and the giraffe ,
the mermaid and the fish,
the cow and the sheep,
my father, the hippopotamus, the horse,
AND the bird AND the bee . . .
as well as with the monkey that sits
oh so high, high, HIGH up
in the old, old, OLD apple tree!

The cat told me she (quite simply)
simply had to agree!
AND so did her best friend, the dog!

The wise old owl told me he had to agree!
AND so did his VERY best friend,
the oh so VERY well dressed FROG!

It really, truly is as we have all heard!
It is up to each AND every one
of us to protect THIS world!
And since life is, after all, really, truly
one very, very, VERY great BIG test!
each AND every one of us
needs to do our very, very, VERY best!
And as to me, and as to you,
this simply is NOT brand new NEWS!
AND we ALL must (quite simply)
simply recycle, re-purpose AND re-use!
And not ONLY that . . .
We need to protect habitats . . . OR . . .
it will be as we have ALL heard
we will ALL go the way of the dodo bird!

And so . . .
tonight when you (like me) go to bed,
remember what my mother said!
She said, "We need to protect
ALL of the creatures of this world,
before we ALL go extinct
like the dodo BIRD!"
So please . . .
recycle, re-purpose and re-use!
AND . . . also please ADD to THAT . . .
please protect each creature's habitat!
Or it will be just as we have ALL heard!
AND we will ALL (quite simply)
simply go the way of
the very, very, VERY extinct dodo bird!

"Wouldn't it be nice if we could see a dodo bird?"

Penelope Dyan

www.ingramcontent.com/pod-product-compliance
Ingram Content Group UK Ltd.
Pitfield, Milton Keynes, MK11 3LW, UK
UKHW060135240426
12048UKWH00002B/46